Count Your Way through
India

by Jim Haskins

illustrations by Liz Brenner Dodson

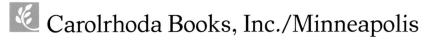 Carolrhoda Books, Inc./Minneapolis

Special thanks to Professors David Kopf and Rocky Miranda, from the Departments of History and Linguistics (respectively) at the University of Minnesota, for their assistance.

LIBRARY OF CONGRESS CATALOGING-IN-PUBLICATION DATA

Haskins, James, 1941–
  Count your way through India / by Jim Haskins ;
illustrations by Liz Brenner Dodson.
      p.   cm.
  Summary: An introduction to the land and people of
India accompanied by instructions on how to read and
pronounce the numbers one through ten in Hindi.
  ISBN 0-87614-414-8 (lib. bdg.)
  1. India—Juvenile literature. [1. India. 2.
Counting.] I. Dodson, Liz Brenner, ill. II. Title.
DS407.H28 1990
954—dc20   89-13925
                                              CIP
                                               AC

Manufactured in the United States of America

1 2 3 4 5 6 7 8 9 10 99 98 97 96 95 94 93 92 91 90

Introductory Note

Over 800 million people live in India. At least 15 major languages and hundreds of different dialects are spoken there. One of the languages used in India is English, which was introduced by the British who ruled parts of India from the 1700s to 1947. Since 1965, the primary official language of India has been Hindi. Hindi is spoken in the northern part of the country, and it is used, along with English, for most government business. Hindi is the language in which we will count our way through India.

The Hindi alphabet is the same as that used for Sanskrit, which is an ancient Indian language. Many sounds used in Hindi are very different from those used in English. One *r* sound in Hindi is pronounced with a slight roll of the tongue against the roof of the mouth. This rolling *r* is represented by two *r*s in the pronunciation guides.

ा एक (ache)

One banyan tree can grow to look like a whole forest. The banyan tree sends down roots from its branches, which are high above the ground. When the roots reach the ground, each of them takes hold in the soil and over time becomes another trunk. In that way, a single tree can have hundreds of trunks and look like a vast forest.

The banyan tree is native to India and to its neighboring countries. One of the most famous banyan trees is located at the Calcutta Botanic Garden. It is more than 200 years old.

२ दो (dough)

There are **two** circles on the flag of India, one inside the other. The circles are part of an ancient Indian symbol called the *Dharma Chakra*, which means "Wheel of Law."

India's legal systems and government have helped bind the nation together since its independence in 1947. Despite all the problems that come with a country that has such a huge and varied population, India remains a democratic nation with a strong respect for the law.

३ तीन (teen)

Mohandas K. Gandhi, who was called the *Mahatma*, or Great Soul, of India, kept only **three** items of furniture: a cot to sleep on, a mat to sit on, and a spinning wheel. Gandhi, a lawyer educated in England, led his people in nonviolent protest against British rule in India during the early to mid 1900s.

Gandhi believed that the Indian people needed to find a way to earn their own money so they would not have to rely on Great Britain for support. One way to achieve this goal was by producing cotton cloth to sell to other countries. So every day, Gandhi spun cotton into thread, which could be made into cloth. Gandhi's spinning wheel became a symbol to his followers of an independent India. Eventually, the Indians reached their goal of independence—in great part due to the efforts of the Mahatma.

Gandhi's philosophy of nonviolent protest was also important in the United States, where it greatly influenced Martin Luther King, Jr., and the nonviolent civil rights movement of the 1960s.

४ चार (charr)

There are **four** tall towers, called *minarets*, at each corner of the *Taj Mahal*—the best-known monument in India. The Taj Mahal is a huge marble tomb, surrounded by gardens and fountains. Its image is reflected in a rectangular pool. Buried inside the tomb are Mumtaz Mahal, who died around 1630 A.D. giving birth to her 14th child, and her husband, the Indian ruler Shah Jahan. When Mumtaz Mahal died, Shah Jahan was heartbroken and ordered that a spectacular monument be built to his wife. It took about 20,000 workers and more than 20 years to finish the Taj Mahal.

५ पाँच (paunch)

The *Diwali*, a Hindu festival of lights, lasts for **five** days. The festival is a joyous ceremony dedicated to Lakshmi, the goddess of wealth and beauty.

For the festival, people put *chirags*, which are red saucers filled with oil and a cotton wick, all around their houses and light them at twilight. The lights are traditionally meant to guide Lakshmi to people's homes with her gifts of good fortune.

Many children float chirags down the Ganges River, which is sacred to Hindus. The children make wishes as their chirags float away. If the chirags remain lit until they are out of sight, the children believe their wishes will come true.

ह छे (chay)

The **six** countries that border India are Pakistan, China, Nepal, Bhutan, Burma, and Bangladesh. The Himalayas, the highest mountain range in the world, form a natural border between India and the countries to its north.

The Himalayas started to form millions of years ago when the landmass of India began pushing up against the larger landmass of Asia. These natural forces are still at work, pushing the mountains nearly two inches (five centimeters) higher each year.

७ सात (sot)

Seven spices commonly used in Indian cooking are coriander, cardamom, turmeric, cumin, cayenne pepper, cinnamon, and ginger. Cooks grind these and other spices daily to get the freshest flavors possible. Although some Indians eat meat, many are vegetarians, and Indian cooks use spices to make vegetable dishes distinctive and highly flavored.

India's strong tradition of vegetarianism is related to the Hindu religion, which is followed by about 80 percent of the nation's population. Hindus believe the soul can take many shapes, including that of an animal. The cow has been a sacred animal to Hindus for thousands of years. Cows are not worshiped, but they may not be killed. Since cows are valued so highly, they are allowed to wander freely and can be seen on city streets.

छ आठ (art)

Eight things you are likely to see on a busy street in a modern Indian city are rickshaws, buses, fortune-tellers, movie posters, cows, vendors, people in Western business suits, and people in traditional Indian clothing.

The cities of India are very crowded, and old traditions and practices exist alongside more modern ways of life. While agriculture is the biggest part of India's economy, India has also constructed satellites and nuclear-powered reactors. A unique mixture of old and new can be found throughout India.

छ   नौ (now)

Of the thousands of wildlife species that inhabit India, **nine** are the Asian elephant, the Himalayan black bear, the Bengal tiger, the Hoolock Gibbon ape, the Indian lion, the red panda, the king cobra, the common kingfisher, and the rare, one-horned Indian rhinoceros.

India has a great variety of animals because the country has many different habitats—from snow-covered mountains to grassy plains, from rain forests to deserts. There have been laws to protect animals in India since 300 B.C. Still, many animals in India have become in danger of dying out. India is trying to save its wildlife from that fate with over 100 wildlife sanctuaries.

१० दस (duss)

    In some Indian drama, the famous Indian villain Ravana takes center stage. Ravana is a **ten**-headed demon who captures Rama's wife, Sita. Rama, who is the hero, must triumph over Ravana to free his wife. The story of Rama, called the *Ramayana*, is long and takes many hours to dramatize.

    India has a strong tradition of drama and entertainment. Millions of Indians go to movies regularly, and India leads the world in the production of feature films.

Pronunciation Guide

1 / एक (ache)

2 / दो (dough)

3 / तीन (teen)

4 / चार (charr)

5 / पाँच (paunch)

6 / छे (chay)

7 / सात (sot)

8 / आठ (art)

9 / नौ (now)

10 / दस (duss)